CLASSIC
decoupage

Design, illustrations and text by Meme Design

TOP THAT!

Copyright © 2003 Top That! Publishing plc,
Top That! Publishing, 27023 McBean Parkway, #408 Valencia, CA 91355
Top That! is a Registered Trademark of Top That! Publishing plc
www.topthatpublishing.com

Contents

Introduction

WELCOME to the fascinating world of decoupage. A world where anyone, even those with very little artistic flair, can create wonderful, individual works of art. Decoupage is simple, inexpensive, and, above all, fun.

Decoupage is the craft of decorating surfaces with cut-out paper shapes or images, then sealing them with varnish. Despite the stunning results this creates, it is remarkably easy and can be tackled by anyone who can wield a pair of scissors and a glue brush. In its simplest form, all you do is cut out pictures, glue them onto an object, and finish off with coats of varnish.

This simple craft can be used to decorate anything from a tiny trinket box to an enormous table. As long as an object has a fairly even surface, it is suitable for decoupage. If you are willing to spend some time on the preparation, you can use decoupage on all kinds of materials, including wood, metal, glass, and plastic.

Most of the decoupage projects in this book are suitable for a beginner. Once you get started, however, you will soon be inspired to experiment with something a little more demanding. Simply take the techniques you find here and adapt them to whatever you have in mind. Decoupage is so relaxing and calming, you may well become addicted. So read through this book and enjoy!

DECOUPAGE has a long and varied history. Its origins can be traced back to many distant lands and times. In twelfth-century China, peasants used paper cut-outs to decorate lanterns, gift boxes, and other everyday items. German and Polish artisans have been using paper cut-outs for decorations for many hundreds of years.

VENETIAN CRAFTSMEN

Decoupage as we know it, however, was developed in seventeenth-century Venice, at a time when Oriental lacquered work was highly fashionable. As demand outstripped supply, cabinet makers began to produce fake lacquerwork, known as *lacca contrafatta* – counterfeit lacquer. At the same time, hand-painted furniture became so expensive that Venetian craftsmen bought engravings and hand-colored them to stick to furniture, instead of employing master painters. This process, known as "poor man's art," was so effective, it spread throughout Europe and the UK. In the eighteenth and nineteenth centuries, it was particularly popular among the genteel women of the French court, who spent many leisurely hours decorating hatboxes, screens, and toiletry objects. It was here that the name "decoupage," derived from the word *découper,* which means "to cut," was coined.

ENGLISH LADIES

In eighteenth-century England, many ladies spent their days decorating objects with cut-out images, then lacquering them. This was generally known as Japanning. Japanning was seen as a refined and worthy activity suitable for gentlewomen in much the same way as intricate embroidery. In 1760, a London printer published a book called *The Ladies Amusement or The Art of Japanning Made Easy.* This book contained over 1,500 images to cut out and color.

VICTORIAN STYLE

Decoupage reached new heights in Victorian England, where it took on a more sentimental, collage style. This was probably influenced by the introduction of greetings cards, floral wallpapers, highly decorative printed papers, and heavy braid trimmings that were used to decorate objects. Although it lacked the subtlety of earlier decoupage, it was certainly considered to be eye-catching, bold, and romantic.

MODERN REVIVAL

Decoupage remains popular today. In fact, in recent years it has experienced something of a revival in America, Japan, and Europe. The exciting new prints produced by modern printing methods make it a simple and inexpensive craft for anyone to enjoy.

Victoriana

THE VICTORIAN ERA (1837-1901) was an exciting time for style and design in the home. Goods, such as floral wallpaper and fabrics, were mass-produced for the first time, and the public couldn't get enough of them. As the new middle-class had money to spend and took huge pride in their homes, distinctive styles began to emerge.

The projects in this book are heavily influenced by the styles and designs of the Victorian era. The Victorian period spanned many decades, and this meant a multitude of different styles. The Victorian age was essentially a time of imitation, when everything from Gothic to Rococo was revived. In fact, Victorian style can be divided into three fairly distinctive periods. The early years saw a Gothic revival in architecture and design. Mid-Victorian style was lush and highly adorned, although the late Victorians rallied against this apparent bad taste with styles such as Art Nouveau, the Celtic Revival, Aestheticism, and The Arts and Crafts movement.

INSPIRATION

So don't feel constrained—any of these styles can be used to imitate Victoriana. Use rich, dark colors, such as ruby reds and forest greens, combined with images of birds and animals and lush fabrics for truly authentic looks. You need look no further than William Morris wallpapers and old Valentine's Day cards for inspiration. Watch out, too, for reproductions of religious and botanical prints. And, as this was an age of exploration and expansion, seek out anything to do with the British Empire.

The Victorians loved to cover everything from linen boxes and screens, to lamp stands and tea caddies, with decoupage. They obviously found it addictive, and you're sure to become hooked, too, once you get started. So, get snipping and sticking and, before you know it, you'll have a totally coordinated home.

Although you can buy specialist supplies, most of the things you need can be found lying around the house.

PAPER IMAGES

You won't have to search far for these. Almost anything made out of paper will do, so start saving newspapers, magazines, wrapping paper, greetings cards, wallpaper, and photographs. Look out for source books and reproduction prints to photocopy and color in. Once you start searching, you will find a limitless supply of material for your decoupage.

GLUES

PVA glue is a white glue that dries to a clear finish. It can be diluted and brushed over a finished project to act as a sealer. Wood glue is also required for some of the projects.

METHYLATED SPIRITS

Methylated spirits is essential for cleaning varnish off your brushes when you have finished.

PAINTS

Latex paints are suitable for most of the projects in this book. White acts as a primer, and colored paint is used as a base coat. Colored inks and watercolor paints are used to color in black and white photocopies. Acrylic paint is also valuable. It comes in a wide range of colors, including metallic.

VARNISH

Oil-based polyurethane and water-based acrylic varnishes are used as a scaler. Polyurethane is tougher, but acrylic doesn't yellow with age. Shellac can be applied to stiffen and seal the paper image.

CARD

Stencil card is needed for some of the projects. If you don't have any, simply opt for a lightweight card. A heavier weight card can also be used. All are available from craft shops.

Equipment

You won't need to buy expensive equipment to begin this fascinating craft. However, here are a few items that you will find useful when creating your decoupage projects.

SCISSORS

You will need a large pair of scissors for bigger jobs, and a small, sharp pair for cutting out more detailed images.

CRAFT KNIFE

A craft knife is useful for cutting out particularly intricate areas, and for scoring through and cutting card.

CUTTING MAT

Always use a cutting mat when using a craft knife. It stops the material slipping and protects the surface underneath.

TWEEZERS

Tweezers are used for picking up and positioning really small pieces of paper.

BRUSHES

You will need various sizebrushes for applying primer and base coats, as well as finer artist brushes for painting color photocopies. PVA glue is best applied with a fine glue brush.

SPONGE

A small sponge is handy for achieving various paint effects.

PENCIL

A sharp pencil is important for marking up designs.

Basic Method

Basic decoupage is very quick and easy to master. Once you've learned the steps here, you will be ready to handle any of the projects in this book. It's best to start with something small and flat.

(1) Prepare the surface. If it's wood, sand and fill in any cracks and prime with latex paint. If it's metal, remove any rust with a proprietary remover and paint with a rust-retardant paint.

(2) Seal the paper image with a coat of shellac. This will stiffen the paper, seal the image, and prevent discoloration.

(3) Cut around the image with small, sharp scissors. Use a craft knife and cutting mat to deal with any really intricate bits.

(4) Arrange the cut-outs on the painted surface. Play around with them until you are happy with the layout, then glue in position. Use tweezers to pick up any particularly delicate pieces.

(5) Paint over the image with a layer of PVA glue. This will help to get rid of any air bubbles and excess glue. Allow to dry.

(6) Seal the design with up to twelve coats of varnish, giving a light sanding between coats. Leave to dry in a well-ventilated, dust-free environment.

Greetings Card

These delightful greetings cards were made from color photocopies taken from a Victorian source book. You could just as easily use scraps of wrapping paper, or images from magazines. A card is easy to make—perfect for beginners.

YOU WILL NEED:

• colored card (6 in. x 8 in.) • a metal ruler
• a pencil • a cutting mat • a craft knife
• photocopies of flower images and a cherub
from a Victorian source book • small, sharp
scissors • PVA glue • a small glue brush

1. Draw a line down the center of the card, then use a craft knife to score down this line and fold it in half.

2. Carefully cut out the flowers using some small scissors and a craft knife.

3. Arrange the flowers in a border around the edges of the card. Once you are happy with the layout, use a small glue brush to stick them down with PVA glue.

4. Open the greetings card and flatten it out on the cutting mat. Use the knife to cut away the middle section to leave a shaped "window."

HANDY TIP!

For a longer-lasting look, you could seal this project with PVA glue or varnish!

5. Cut out the cherub image, or another image of your choice, and glue it onto the inside of the card so that it can be seen through the window.

6. Make a matching envelope by sticking a cherub on the flap.

Picture Frame

Photocopies of images taken from Victorian fashion books are an excellent source of decoupage material. This project uses fan designs to create a highly decorative and unique picture frame. However, numerous other designs would work just as well.

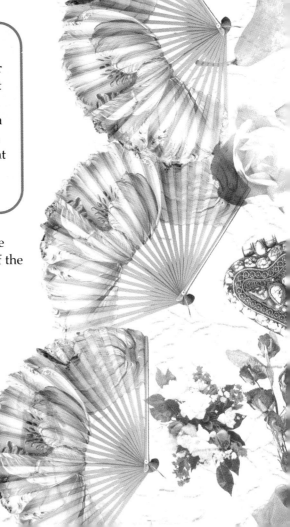

YOU WILL NEED:

- a mounting board (or similar thickness card) • a cutting mat • a metal ruler • a craft knife • paintbrushes • scraps from a Victorian source book • small, sharp scissors • pink latex paint • a glue brush • PVA glue • satin acrylic varnish

The shape of the "window" on the frame is cut to follow the shape of the scraps—this design features fans.

(1) Use the metal ruler and the scalpel to cut out two rectangles of mounting board, both the same size. One of the rectangles is for the front of the frame, and one is for the back.

2 Prime the front and back of the frame with pink latex paint and leave to dry.

3 Use the small, sharp scissors to cut out your chosen images (in this case, the fans).

4 Arrange the images in a frame shape on one of the rectangles of card, slightly overlapping them as you work. Once you are happy with the layout, use a small brush to glue them into position.

5 Brush PVA glue over the top and leave to dry.

6 Make the frame stand by cutting out a triangle from mounting board. Score a horizontal line down the triangle, $1/2$ in. from the tip. Glue this to the back section of the picture frame, as seen below.

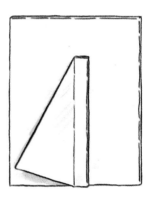

FOR SOMETHING A LITTLE DIFFERENT

Try making a more substantial frame from MDF. Cut out the back and front panels using a jigsaw (not forgetting to wear a face mask as you do so). Then cut out three thin strips of MDF and glue them down the sides and

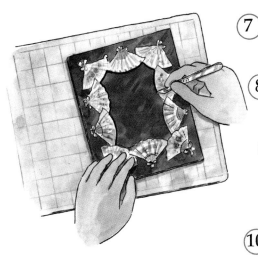

7. Cut out the middle from the front section of the frame to make a shaped window.

8. Turn the frame over and use a small brush to spread glue along three of the edges.

9. Glue the front of the frame to the back. One side should be left open so that your chosen picture can be slipped in.

10. Seal the whole frame with two coats of satin acrylic varnish and allow to dry.

bottom edge of the back panel. Cut a window in the front panel. Then, glue your images in position on the front of the frame, folding them over the edges to get a neat finish. Glue the two panels together, leaving a space at the top to slot in the picture. Finally, varnish the frame to seal it.

Christmas Decorations

It's hard to believe that these gorgeous Christmas decorations are simply made from blown chicken eggs and scraps of paper. Used to decorate your Christmas tree, they will help to create a really traditional "Victorian-feel" Christmas.

1. Use a pin to prick a hole in both ends of the shell of a raw egg. Wiggle the pin around in one end to make the hole slightly larger.

2. Hold the egg over a glass, with the larger hole at the bottom. Blow through the hole in the top of the egg. Keep blowing until all of the yolk and egg white has been blown out. Leave the shell to dry out overnight.

3. Poke a toothpick into the egg, and put the other end into some sticky putty to hold it still. Then, prime the egg with white latex paint and leave it to dry.

4. Use small scissors, or craft knife, to cut out your chosen two images for each egg. Make a few tiny snips around the edges to help them lie flat on the curve of the egg once they are stuck down.

FOR SOMETHING A LITTLE DIFFERENT

You could, alternatively, make Christmas tree decorations by cutting out shapes such as bells, stars, or angels from card (old Christmas cards or cereal boxes are ideal). Cover these with your images in the same way as

5 You could either cover the egg entirely or, alternatively, choose just two images to place on opposite sides of the eggshell. If you only place two images you will need to paint the eggshell with two colored coats after the first coat of latex paint, but make sure it is completely dry before adding the images.

6 Use a small glue brush to glue an image onto each side of the egg.

7 Seal with two to four coats of satin acrylic varnish, and leave to dry.

8 Glue a colorful, narrow ribbon around the egg. Press firmly to make sure it is properly stuck down, then tie a knot at the top and make a loop to hang it by.

you did for the eggshell, making sure you cover the card with white latex paint first. Complete your decorations by applying two to four coats of satin acrylic varnish.

Pencil Holder

Make an attractive pencil holder from a humble tin can and photocopies of old reproduction prints. This one has a tropical bird theme, but you could always choose a theme appropriate to the person it's being made for. If it's for a golf enthusiast, for example, choose golfing images; if it's to be given to a sailor, look for suitable yachting images.

YOU WILL NEED:

- a clean tin can, with the label removed • coarse and fine-grain emery paper • paintbrushes
- white latex paint • green and gold latex paint • photocopies of reproduction bird prints
- small, sharp scissors
- a glue brush • PVA glue
- satin acrylic varnish
- a paper towel

1 Use coarse emery paper to smooth any sharp edges on the tin can, particularly around the top. Then prepare the can inside and out by rubbing it down with fine-grain emery paper.

2 Prime the tin can with white latex paint inside and out. Leave to dry.

3 Paint over the primer with dark green latex paint. Leave to dry.

4 Dab a dry sponge in gold latex paint. Wipe off any excess on a paper towel. Sponge over the green latex paint.

5 Use the small, sharp scissors to cut out the images of your choice (in this case parrots and leaves).

FOR SOMETHING A LITTLE DIFFERENT

Use decoupage to make a whole set of matching desk accessories. You could try decorating a letter rack, a paperweight, or an in-tray. In fact,

6. Use a small glue brush to stick the images in position with PVA glue.

7. Brush a coat of PVA glue over the images to ensure that they are firmly stuck down. Leave to dry.

8. Seal with two to four coats of satin acrylic varnish.

you could even go so far as to decorate an entire desktop to match!
Once you start, the possibilities are endless.

Photo Album

This eye-catching photo album has a nostalgic, seaside theme, making it particularly suitable for all those vacation snaps. As well as decoupage, it is decorated with a simple striped stencil.

YOU WILL NEED:
- a cardboard-covered photo album
- a small paint brush
- white latex paint
- a sponge
- navy and light blue latex paint
- a pencil
- stencil card or thin card
- a craft knife
- a cutting mat
- masking tape
- a small sponge
- small, sharp scissors
- seaside images from a Victorian source book
- PVA glue
- a small glue brush
- satin acrylic varnish

(1) Prime the back and front of your album with white latex paint. Leave to dry.

(2) Use a sponge to cover the primer with navy blue latex paint. Leave to dry.

(3) Cut a piece of stencil card, or thin card, the same size as the album cover.

(4) Draw some wide stripes onto your stencil card.

(5) Cut out the stencil using the craft knife and a cutting mat.

(6) Place the stencil on the photo album, and hold in place with masking tape.

HANDY TIP!

Strips of masking tape could be used instead of a stencil if you find it hard to keep the stencil card in place when applying the latex paint.

FOR SOMETHING A LITTLE DIFFERENT

Although this photo album has a traditional Victorian feel, you might wish to go for something a little more contemporary. Look in magazines and on

7 Dab the sponge into the lighter blue latex paint and wipe off any excess. Then, dab the paint onto the stencil. Allow the paint to partially dry, then remove the stencil. Put aside until it's completely dry.

8 Meanwhile, use the small, sharp scissors to cut out lots of seaside images.

9 Use the small glue brush to glue the images inside the "border." Brush a layer of PVA glue over the top. Leave to dry, then varnish with satin acrylic varnish.

postcards for modern seaside images, or even go for something with an abstract design.

Mirror, Mirror

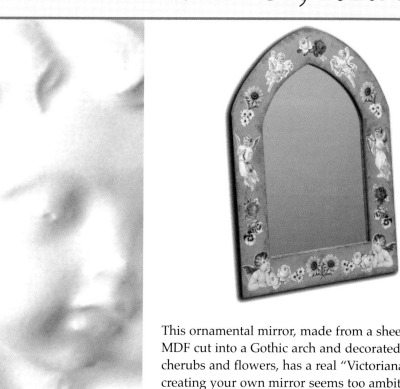

This ornamental mirror, made from a sheet of MDF cut into a Gothic arch and decorated with cherubs and flowers, has a real "Victoriana" feel. If creating your own mirror seems too ambitious, why not buy a plain wood-framed mirror and decorate it yourself?

YOU WILL NEED:
- a rectangular mirror (8 in. x 12 in.)
- a ruler
- a pencil
- a sheet of MDF (11 in. x 15 in.)
- a jigsaw
- a face mask
- wood glue
- a sponge
- white latex paint
- blue and dark blue latex paint
- two paint brushes
- a paper towel
- small, sharp scissors
- Victorian cherubs and flower
- a small glue brush
- PVA glue
- a screwdriver
- double-sided sticky pads
- satin acrylic varnish
- picture rings and chain

(1) Place the mirror on the sheet of MDF and draw around it. Add a $1/2$ in. border to the sides and bottom and draw a Gothic arch at the top, as shown.

(2) Put on your face mask and use the jigsaw to cut out the arch.

③ Draw a second guideline (complete with arch) at least an inch in from the outer edge of the frame and $1/2$ in. from the original outline of the mirror tile. Use the jigsaw to cut this center section out.

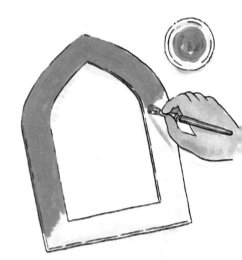

④ Prime the wooden mirror frame with white latex paint and leave to dry.

⑤ Cover the primer with blue latex paint and allow to dry.

FOR SOMETHING A LITTLE DIFFERENT

If using MDF seems a little daunting, you could use very thick cardboard. Use a set square to mark out accurate right-angled corners. Cut it out with

---

(7) Use the small, sharp scissors to cut out lots of cherub and flower images.

(8) Arrange the images around the mirror frame, and glue into position once you are happy with the layout. Leave to dry. Cover the frame with several coats of varnish.

(9) Secure the mirror into position at the back of the frame using double-sided sticky pads.

(6) Dab a dry sponge into the darker blue latex paint. Wipe off any excess on a piece of paper towel. Sponge over the blue latex paint. Allow to dry.

(10) Use a screwdriver to attach two picture rings and a chain to the wooden frame at the back of the mirror.

a sharp craft knife. But be *very* careful to ensure that the knife doesn't slip! Use glue to fix the mirror and cardboard together and the sticky pads to secure the mirror to the wall, providing that the mirror is not too heavy.

Trinket Boxes

These highly decorative trinket boxes have been created by covering basic wooden boxes with color photocopies taken from a Victorian source book. You can buy boxes like these in craft shops, or keep an eye out for old boxes at garage sales, and in junk shops or charity shops.

YOU WILL NEED:
- flower pictures
- small, sharp scissors
- a craft knife • a cutting mat
- a paintbrush • white latex paint • colored latex paint
- PVA glue • small glue brush
- satin acrylic varnish

(1) Carefully cut out the flowers using small, sharp scissors and a craft knife.

(2) Prime the trinket box with a coat of white emulsion. Leave to dry.

37

(3) Cover with two coats of colored latex paint. Leave to dry.

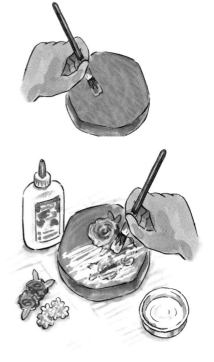

(4) Glue the cut-out flowers in position using PVA glue. Brush a layer of the glue over the top of each cut-out to ensure that they are lying flat. Leave to dry.

(5) Once the PVA glue is dry apply another layer.

FOR SOMETHING A LITTLE DIFFERENT

Decoupage is an excellent way of decorating all sorts of boxes. However, you must always remember to prepare them thoroughly. Wood must be

(6) Finish with a coat of satin acrylic varnish.

While decoupage is strongly associated with Victorian images, don't restrict your work to just these images. Children love having various boxes to store things in, so why not use some wrapping paper featuring their favorite characters?

You could even take this one step further and decorate their desk and closet— they're sure to be the only people in their class with personalized furniture!

sanded down and filled, while metal must be rust-free and primed.Try decorating cookie cans to give a coordinated look in your kitchen.

Decoupage is a great way of customizing new coasters and table mats, or even rejuvenating old ones. The examples here have been decorated with butterflies and flowers photocopied from a source book, but could just as easily be decorated with something a little less feminine.

YOU WILL NEED:

- coasters and table mats, or cake bases about $1/4$ in. deep (11 in. diameter for table mats, and 5 in. diameter for coasters)
- paintbrushes • a sponge
- multipurpose primer • moss green and brown latex paint
- black and white photocopied pictures of butterflies and flowers • shellac • PVA glue
- watercolor paints or colored inks
- small, sharp scissors
- clear polyurethane varnish

(1) Prime the table mats or coasters with multipurpose primer and leave to dry.

(2) Paint the table mats with green latex paint and leave to dry.

3 Sponge watery brown latex paint over the top of this for a textured finish. Leave to dry.

4 Paint black and white photocopies of your chosen design with watercolors. Leave to dry.

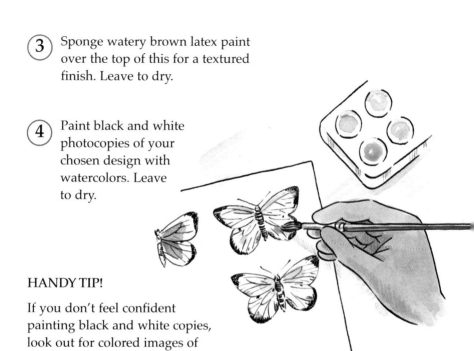

HANDY TIP!

If you don't feel confident painting black and white copies, look out for colored images of butterflies and flowers.

FOR SOMETHING A LITTLE DIFFERENT

Place a single Chinese image in the center of your table mat and decorate the border with an intricate motif for a traditional Oriental look.

(5) Paint over with shellac to "age" and seal.

(6) Cut out the pictures with small, sharp scissors, and arrange on the mats. When you are happy with the layout, secure with PVA glue. Brush a layer of glue over the top.

(7) When completely dry, add up to ten coats of clear polyurethane varnish, leaving it to dry thoroughly between coats.

Try a combination of decoupage and stenciling. Or use photographs of your family to create a constant reminder of your nearest and dearest!

Give an old drinks tray a new lease of life with a
dash of paint and some scraps of wrapping paper.
This particular tray is made out of wood, but
there's no reason why you can't apply decoupage
to a metal or even a plastic one.

YOU WILL NEED:
• an old tray • fine sandpaper
• paintbrushes
• white latex paint • black and
gold latex paint • small, sharp
scissors • floral wrapping paper
• a small glue brush • PVA glue
• clear polyurethane
matt varnish

1. Sand down an old wooden tray until the surface is smooth.

2. Prime with white latex paint and leave to dry.

③ Brush black paint over the primer and allow to dry.

④ Dab a dry paintbrush in the gold paint. Paint several strokes onto some scrap paper until the color looks really soft, then apply paint to the tray with quick strokes. You should end up with a "distressed" look. Practice on paper until you feel confident. Also brush some gold paint into the corners and around the edges of the tray.

⑤ Use small, sharp scissors to cut out some large flowers and leaves from the wrapping paper.

6) Arrange the flowers and leaves on the tray. When you're happy with the positioning, secure with PVA glue. Brush a layer of PVA over the top and leave to dry.

7) Seal with twelve coats of clear polyurethane matt varnish.

Note: Decoupage items are for decorative purposes only and you should avoid surfaces coming into direct contact with food.

Over to You!

BY NOW YOU ARE ALMOST CERTAINLY A DECOUPAGE ADDICT.

So where do you go from here? Well, the sky's the limit. We have only used decoupage on small, everyday objects in this book. However, decoupage was traditionally used to decorate far larger items, and there's no reason why you can't do the same now you've mastered the basic skills.

Look around your home for items that need rejuvenating—anything from a large screen to a chest is suitable. You can even use decoupage to create a totally unique toilet seat and toilet paper holder! And don't forget the finer details: accessorize the smaller household items in your house by making unique doorknobs and light pulls.

Don't restrict yourself to Victoriana. Modern images work just as well. Branch out and experiment with anything paper that appeals to you. Geometric and abstract designs look great. In fact, virtually anything works—even stamps and old product labels!